Letters from the Gardeners Cottage Volume 3

SL SOURWINE

www.SLSourwine.com

CONTENTS

MAY 2021

Argyll's Secret Coast
Scotland, UK

May 26, 2021

Greetings dear hearts!

It won't surprise you at all to hear that I've been thinking about things a lot this month. It's interesting to me that the more I am doing things I like and love and that feel valuable to me, the more ideas and connections and creations keep coming. If you've ever had the worry that you might be a one

I realised I hadn't shown you the completion of my floor efforts in the glasshouse for this year. I love it so much and spend most morning coffee times in here before I do anything.

trick pony and have procrastinated doing *that thing* because you worry it will be the only thing. It's definitely been my experience that it only takes a little bit of movement in the direction of your creativity and the waters start to shift and flow and next thing you know you have almost more than a lifetime's worth of things you could do. I always used to marvel at authors who wrote such different and prolific works. I would question how did they manage to be done with one enough to move onto the next? I'm noticing now that the pull moves you onwards. It's why some ideas are for a particular time too—like a spot on a bank you pass in a boat or one of those historical view point markers on a highway. You either stop or you don't, but they aren't portable experiences in time. I used to never have time for those look outs. I find myself much more often curious now that I've turned down so much of my mind's internal hurry factory settings!

May is also the first month I've had visitors and even a hug from a friend in a very long time. It was bloody wonderful. My friend and former neighbour Bridget came up from down south for a few days before I wrote this. And shortly after I will be expecting a couple of friends and their children for almost a whole week. It feels so very nice to have people back. The process of waking the house up has been a gift too. As my friend and patron Gail calls it "tickling things awake." Bridget and her little dog Toby, who Alfred basically grew up with, were such a gentle return to all the best things about time with people you care about. We walked and talked and cooked and gardened and napped! It was really wonderful. She was also here while I received my first COVID vaccination. We planned it out incase I got ill, but luckily I just had a little evening fever and that was it. So lucky. And it feels wonderful to get to take my first step in helping all of us protect each other.

The Weather and Gratitude for Glasshouses

May has been most strange. So hot. So cold. So dry. Violently wet. A lot of the vegetable plants have been flowering very early and at first it felt like they were so confused. Now I think they know more than we do and I should have let them get on with it. Who knows what is coming next!

I feel so fortunate to have so much protected gardening space in the glasshouse. Right now the jasmine vine is in full bloom and the aroma is so powerful. Someone described the scent as "heavy and thick." I like that. The kind of scent you can trust to push out all the others. There is no need to press your face close to her flowers. Stand back and let her envelop you. It's wonderful.

All sorts of things are coming on and some have needed very careful tending. It comes back to that thinking I was doing... I was thinking about what we tend in our lives, consciously and unconsciously. The very intentional tending that happens as you try to grow vegetables and flowers from seed to harvest. The unintentional tending I do when I don't speak up so someone else stays comfortable or how I tend an idea of myself that maybe no longer suits my life. It's interesting things to think about while watering tomatoes!

I'm growing some things this year that I have never tried before. I've got camomile, feverfew, cosmos, phlox, sweet potatoes and even courgettes (zucchini) which I haven't grown myself. Plants you aren't yet familiar with how they look and act at different stages and always wonder if you are doing the right things. It's the kind of drama I can stand these days.

I've put all my tools away in the shed and have set the glasshouse up for growing and enjoyment only for the rest of the summer. To luxuriate in it as a space, not just a work in progress. This is a new behaviour for me and I think I like it.

I even managed to get my first outside bed built and plants in. The weather for the next week or so looks very warm and sunny, so if not now then when?! LOL. Everything feels like a bit of a gamble this year, but having my long history in the horse racing world before coming to Scotland, that's not as uncomfortable for me as others sometimes I think.

Around the Estate

Spring has been in fits and starts. The trees have taken forever to leaf, and then all of a sudden, like they couldn't wait another second they were here and the veil of green has descended and you have to work a little harder for your views.

So many of the fruit trees had blossoms tossed away by the wind. It will be interesting to see where that leaves us for fruiting later. Just before this letter goes off I found the first hawthorn blossoms of the year and as it does, your heart just releases a little ancestral tension and you know you made it through another winter. They continue. All will be well.

A combination of factors like a lot of desk work, my knee still not being better, and returning to work in the gallery have meant I wasn't walking as far afield every day as I was used to doing. But I tended my connection to this landscape by things like spending 10 minutes filming a starfish hunting a snail in a tide pool; trying to take the perfect picture of a bluebell (impossible); and eating wood violets and sorrel on each of my walks no matter how short to have some of the land itself as part of me. It's a good practise with plants you know for sure you can eat.

The bluebells are so much later here than in England so at the moment they are in that full wonder before disappearing. Just as it's so hard to take their picture, as soon as you start relying on them to be there for you on your pathways, that you will always have your footsteps dusted in mists of blue... well they disappear and you very much hope to see them again next year.

Another spring phenomenon that I hadn't witnessed before was captured this month. One evening Alfred and I went down to Ardmarnoch Bay by the boathouse and I noticed the most amazing thing. It must have been limpet breeding season (a marine mollusc which has a cone shaped shell and clings tightly to rocks). It stood out because every surface available, whether it was a shell, a rock, or a piece of seaweed, was covered in the most perfect rows of tiny tiny limpets. It was like someone had gone through the bay with a dot pen and decorated every surface. It took me a while to understand what I was seeing, but then I was on my knees attempting to photograph a sample of it for you. These lovely shells do the trick I think. It was so geometrically perfect and on so many surfaces. I was in awe of nature once again.

The butterflies have returned in a lovely way now adding such a bopping about energy to the bees and the birds. My little robin is only spotted now every once in a while. Hopefully it's off growing into a marvellous creature with all the skills for a long life. The swallows are back (as you can see from your envelopes this month) and that brings another way of moving into the yard. Swooping and gliding and diving. They are impossible so far to capture in flight. The little wrens have indeed nested in the jasmine in the glasshouse, what sensible property choices!!! I will try and sneak a camera up to spy on them for our next letter.

The gorse and the blue to make you swoon.

All is well really besides the fact that I desperately need a haircut! I hope it has been a good month for you too. I so appreciate you for being here and your support.
Lots of love,

Susie

xx

JUNE 2021

The Gardeners Cottage
Argyll's Secret Coat
Scotland, UK

Barely June, 2021

My dearest friends,

I'm not sure I've ever described to you what it feels like to have you out there waiting for a letter from me. It's the most wonderful thing. Like each day and each walk and each flower or creature or resting has a bit of a purpose beyond what it means to me personally. There's a bit of

The stunning Ragged Robin. Part of the Carnation family, it is native to Europe and loves boggy wetlands.

magic and a lot of tapping into my own creativity as I do it. That's where the learning lies for me, because it's my own creativity only for my purpose and in the last two years that is something I have come to understand isn't as easy to hold as when it's for someone else. This month in particular has reminded me to measure the size of the cups of my creative essence I am using for other projects, other people, even this place, and remember to tend to my own always first. Whoops. This month was such a lesson in that. That's why your letters are so late. Mid-month I thought I could do all the things. And I couldn't.

So a couple of pieces of clear learning to share.

1. Sometimes you need help. I had absolutely no ability to even imagine a painting this month. And I knew if I waited for that to be different I'd miss the month completely! So I paid another artist for the adorable little lamb photo that is poking out of your retro air-mail envelopes I was so delighted to order this month to shake things up. I hope it brought you the same smile it brought to me. Back to paintings next month!
2. Sometimes you have to make decisions for yourself knowing there might be repercussions and that's ok. I knew by being late I might lose some of you, particularly the folks who were relatively new to the letters. And that is ok. I did break trust. It's ok if there is a cost to that. It's not ok if I hurt myself to make money anymore. I write about that so much and when those decisions come closer to the skin than just an idea it is more difficult, but for me even more essential to choose correctly. So I won't hide that from you either, that it's still hard for my people-pleasing side, I hope everyone likes me forever and ever. To put my self first to take those kinds of actions (or delayed action in this case). It's worth it.

Please get help when you need it. In all ways. It can be as simple as investing in support for things that aren't helping you bringing your beautiful, unique energy and creation into the world, or getting help with things that prevent you showing up for loving the people around you. I'm happy to wear the same old clothes most days and have someone clean my house. Your version will look different to you. I don't know for sure, but I think this is one of the keys to changing the world systems that have been created to extract versus add.

It has been the most stunning month here on the west coast of Scotland. The first weeks saw the the misty-blue footpaths of bluebells disappear into the bright green bracken as it shot up by the foot a day it felt like. There were drifts of hawthorn blossom across the hillsides. I can't tell you how beautiful they were this year.

The Hawthorn tree nearest my house.

I've never seen it like this and although hawthorn doesn't have a reputation for being a sought out scent, I can tell you that the heavy sweetness of the blossoms lingered on the paths and roads and you literally walked into it and through it. It was divine to me. I think we are so used to scent that we create and place that we forget sometimes how much better at it nature can be than us! I went on specific walks to meet as many hawthorn trees as I could while they were obviously celebrating their good fortune this spring! It was like a hawthorn festival! Hawthorn is medicine for the heart and I'm pretty grateful for this demonstration that our hearts can be tended this year after such a hard time through lock downs.

I'm filling the letter this month with flowers. The wild and cultivated wonders that filled my camera this June. I fell in love with everything this month (so unusual for me I know LOL) and in the bright light and long twilights its was impossible not to take "just one more" picture trying to capture them perfectly.

A wild Orchid.

I think I took a million pictures of foxglove in all sorts of light, videos of them swaying in the breeze and bees crawling straight into their beautiful bell shaped flowers. I know the sound of a bee deep in a foxglove now and I love that about my life.

What is it about humans and flowers? I'm curious for theories. Would it have been because their blossoms indicated our successful transverse of the winter months and that the availability and plenty of food comes with

The bee's favourite Foxglove.

them? Is it just a deep connection to beauty and appreciation of it through the ways our particular eyes see? We know different species see the world entirely differently. Do they love flowers or find beauty in other shapes?

I kept finding new species (some of which I did not manage to photograph well). The wet start and then the warmth of June I think let some dormant faces take centre stage this month. Some of my favourites were the lovely Ragged Robin at the top of the letter. A second species of wild orchid called a Bell orchid that is deep maroon in colour. Another boggy ground dweller called Cross Leaf Heath or Bog Heather which looks like a pink dandelion with scales! The tiny white flowers of common Marsh Bedstraw —which once upon a time would have been collected to stuff mattresses because of its sweet smell. The thistles, the irises, the vetch, the arrival of the first sweet peas and of course my delight in the ranunculus that have lived up to all the billing as the prettiest of the pretty.

In the Glasshouse

The smartest thing I did was commit to having the raspberries in the glasshouse for their second year. I was eating fresh berries from mid-June and it hasn't stopped yet. The strawberries were quick to join in fruiting and most days right now include a handful of berries with break-fast, plus some others while I'm out watering through out the day!

Salad leaves are all coming from home now and the cucumbers have finally agreed to grow on. I can't wait to have all my favourite ingredients from outside the kitchen door! My cherry tomatoes after their very weird, slow start are finally beginning to fruit. The Paul Robeson heirlooms are HUGE but not ripened yet. So all is eager anticipation around here. The basil is ready and the dill! I'll have to keep seeding them so they remain ready when the main acts decide to join us too!

The peas have as always delivered with joy. I'm about to seed one more set to finish the summer. I put some others out in the experimental outdoor garden and they are doing quite well at the moment too. Our problem with flooding out there has been non- existent obviously with the lack of rain, but who knows what July will bring. It's been very wet in the south so a small change of jet stream and we could be swamped like last July! You can only wait to see.

The ability to unhook even that little bit from the plastic wrapped veg of the supermarket is so satisfying. I'm getting better with each passing year with understanding just how much of what I need to grow to actually make a dent in using it. The courgettes are really taking off and I'm pretty sure my two plants

will deliver more than enough for me to eat and make things to store too.

Also speaking of anticipation the apricots are large and just starting to turn. By the time I write you next I hope to be deep into enjoying and processing their loveliness. Fingers crossed.

Company!

The greatest joys of the last month have been visits from actual friends! Oh my goodness it was good to welcome them back into the cottage. Go to restaurants. Hug them!!! I had my first vaccination this month which was also a relief and delight. (Can't wait for the second). It was just the loveliest thing to prepare for each set. Although I forgot how much laundry is involved! LOL

There were lots of adventures including my first visit to the island of Bute. It was gorgeous. I loved it. Beautiful views back to the Cowal Peninsula (where I live) and across the Clyde to the mainland. I learned about a sad, special place there called Canada Hill which was where people came to stand and get the last glimpse of the ships carrying their loved ones away to Canada. Ships like the one that carried my great grandfather from Gourock on the Empire Visa. Economic migrants leaving their family and homes, most often for ever, to assist in the colonisation and extraction of wealth from Canada on behalf of the Empire. The sadness is so magnified for me these days understanding more of how these people's lives were used to advance agendas not for their own benefit as they were told. Replace the farming people of Scotland with sheep for economic gain. Replace the indigenous people of Canada with tenant farmers from here to send wealth back here to build these beautiful homes and estates. The losses and cost of these ideas was extraordinary. I don't think we will ever heal as a society until we also recognise the harm this caused not only to the people colonised but those who were used to do it.

Things were light and heavy this month! On Solstice I was alone and declined the opportunity to create a celebration with some of the other women who live on the estate. Sometimes it can feel like it would just be performative unless I was willing to be the container of the space. I didn't feel like I had that capacity, so I kept to myself. I took a leisurely early evening walk. I gathered wild flowers on the way. What came to me most was not the joy and fertility and riches of summer, but a remembering of the people of this landscape. All those lost and taken. All the feet over all the time. I just felt like it was for them this year. So I left my offering on the standing stone and went home full of gratitude for my life.

Much love,
Susie
xx

In early June the world of leaf and blade and flowers explodes,
and every sunset is different.
- John Steinbeck.

JULY 2021

The Gardeners Cottage
Argyll's Secret Coast
Scotland, UK

July 25, 2021

Dear friend,

After last month I immediately started working on the
envelopes for July so that we
would return to normal this
month. I'm so pleased I did.
It's funny how sometimes

Albertine roses.

when we let up the pressure we can shoot forward so quickly! I
have found that my little changes based on the lessons the
universe was dolling out last month have really been helping.

I'm preparing and planning for an exciting month of writing
and (finally) promoting the book edition of Letters from The
Gardeners Cottage! Although it's been available to order on line
I haven't done any of the work in getting it out there. The
lovely thing is that it has even sold a few copies each month
even with me not helping it at all. So I'm very excited to say
that it August will be all about that for me. If you were one of
the folks that took the book as a bonus last year if you have
time or inclination I'd love if you visited Amazon or Good Reads
and reviewed it. I'd be very grateful. But no obligation as I'm
the most grateful that writing to you made it possible at all.

Three if by Sea

I had the most exciting kind of visitors this month—the kind that arrive by sea! Friends of friends Debs and Neil are circumnavigating the UK this year in their lovely wooden sailboat Galago. I was happy to issue a dinner invite and suggestions for mooring for a calm night's sleep. When not aboard they live in Worthing (where I moved to Scotland from) and it turns out we had indeed met before! We met at the January swim that started my year of wild swimming when I joined a group down at the beach there. Both Debs and I lost our favourite wool hats to the very strong sea that day!

Watching them come in across the loch from Tarbert under sail on a warm summer evening was such a stunning scene. Their boat that night is the one which inspires the envelopes this month. Debs' father was aboard with them for this leg of the trip and I hosted them all for dinner in the glasshouse. We had the most perfect of times and one of those kinds of unplanned evenings that you'll never forget. They moored overnight in Ardmarnock Bay before making their way through the Crinan Canal to begin to wind their way through the Hebrides. They left home in April and intend to be away through November. What an adventure!! I gifted them a small strawberry plant for their herb window aboard.

I often stand at the side of the loch listening to all the things that can be heard, the human things. When the wind is coming in gently from the west you can hear all sorts of things. For example today there was a bang and popping and I could have sworn our estate guys were shooting down towards the water. But when I arrived I realised it was coming from across the loch! You can hear traffic on the highway on the other side sometimes. You can definitely hear people on their boats. It's one of the advantages of walks by yourself because you aren't really chatting to yourself (too much) so you learn how far sound carries here quickly.

Yesterday afternoon I upset an oystercatcher with my presence on the beach at low tide. It's cries echoed so loudly agains the bared stone and amplified it at least 20x what it actually was. So this of course makes me think about the days when this area was a thriving kingdom and what someone like me would have been watching and hearing on the loch. It made me remember the story of the viking ship invasion at Otter Ferry just north of here. What would it have looked and sounded like to watch hundreds of viking ships go by? Did they all go by?

I found a lovely recording of one of the stories of that battle and I realised that although I can't play it for you in a letter, I can make a code that you can scan and get taken straight to it! It's worth trying out.

Open your camera on your phone.

Hold it over the sheet like you were going to take a picture of the code.

Wait for your phone to give you a notification that says "open forestryandland.gov.cot"

Tap it and enjoy the 6 minute story!

If that doesn't work for you, you can just search for Viking Invasion of Otter Ferry and the story by Patsy Dyer. I hope you enjoy.

In the Glasshouse and Gardens

Approaching high summer in this part of the world means it's fruit harvesting time! That time of year when all the jars taking up space in the cupboard are put to use and more (how could that not be enough??).

I'm trying to do a little bit each day to see just where I can get. I've managed to already gift my neighbours with the first set of the apricot jam and it is perhaps even more wonderful than usual.

Here's what has been going on:

Cherries having the year of their lives. Bigger. Juicier. More of them. I've got one large and one small cherry pie filling in the freezer. Ate one with my yogurt for two weeks straight. And I've managed a wonderful lot through the dehydrator. I want to keep up on some more of that. I know that if in January or March if I can pull some dried cherries out and throw them in my breakfast or some scones or buns I'll be thrilled.

Black currants again had a good year. I have taught everyone the value of home made creme de cassis! I made a really big batch of black currant chutney that is very vinegary at the moment. I hope it mellows. I made a small batch of jam which was perfect so might regret my choices there.

Apricots! If you've been here a while you know that this is my favourite thing. When I moved here I really liked the idea of having an apricot tree, but I had no idea what that would do to me in reality. My life revolves around anticipation and then enjoyment of the apricots. After last year's big prune the tree still managed a glorious crop this year. Also thanks to the early arrival of the bees. Some of the apricots are as big as apples! I've put up some brandy, did the first round of jam and dehydrating, and have shared with the neighbours. And there are so many to go yet. I'm so thrilled. Guests coming this weekend have no idea that they are going to help with making jam and prepping fruit basically.

Gooseberries. I'm not very versed in gooseberries. For example I had to look up the fact that there are in fact red and white/green ones because I was very confused about harvesting. There is a whole lot of them in the orchard at the moment so I may take some of them on. I don't think it's going to be a very good year for apples so it is probably wise to do as much with the berries as possible.

Lovely peaches this summer.

Peaches. I never expect much from the peach trees, but even this year after my vicious little prune to try and get them back towards the shape they need to be to live and thrive in the glasshouse long term, well low and behold the warm weather has delivered some beautiful peaches to be. They aren't quite ripe yet, but they are gorgeous and are earmarked for eating straight from the tree.

It's at this time of year that I am am deeply grateful for the planters of food trees and bushes. Those whose foresight reaches decades into the future. So here I am, someone they could never have imagined, am able to unplug from the plastic productivity of the supermarket fruit industry for a few months completely. And if I'm thoughtful, much less throughout the whole year. I think about the unintended consequences/ benefits of their decision a lot. And I spend a lot of time thinking about what I am contributing in this way too. For the moment though it is my season for receiving the goodness and abundance of their co-creation with nature. And it's wonderful.

Fresh Loch Fyne mackerel delivery!

My neighbour came down the other night with a mackerel that he had caught out in the loch. Out of the water for a couple of hours, cleaned and twenty minutes to my dinner. (Stuffed with garlic and lemon and rubbed with olive oil, parsley, salt & pepper). He carried it down to me in his hand. I treasure every episode of ways the food miles are shortening in my life. It makes me want more of that for everyone. It shouldn't be a luxury or aspirational.

And I could not leave you without mentioning the roses. Oh my the roses have been completely at their peak this month. The fragrance coming off the, now identified as Albertine (thank you Ann!), rose at my front door and the Poet's Wife in the glasshouse truly flavoured my month. Thank goodness the sweet peas have decided to come on now to replace them. How lucky am I to walk in this perfumed world most of my days? I have taken cuttings to see whether or not I will be successful in multiplying this goodness and sharing it. My accidental cutting of the Poet's Wife rose (I dropped a pruning into the ground cover and it was moist enough to root!) Is doing well in its pot and is about to graduate to the next size. Exciting times for me!

Much love,
Susie
xx

AUGUST 2021

The Gardeners Cottage
Argyll's Secret Coast
Scotland, UK

August 25, 2021

Dear friends,

It's a completely perfect evening here at The Cottage
tonight. I'm sitting on the patio outside the guest room just
listening to all the bees and the breeze in the big trees beside
me. There's just enough to bring the smell of sweet peas to me
every couple of minutes. It's been one of those highly pleasant
days where it's kind of impossible to go inside as much as you
need to. I've found myself perched on stairs and moving chairs
into the shade and checking the laundry and just generally
being called outside. I hope you know the kind of days I'm
talking about. They only seem to come near the end of summer,
or maybe I just heed their call more at this time of year knowing there might not be too many more.

The beginning of August was wet and cold and you would
have thought autumn would be upon us very soon. But instead
it warmed again in quite unexpected ways and nothing is going
quietly just yet. Including me.

This month was my 50th birthday. A number unimaginable
to my younger self in a way, but completely indifferent to my
present self. I told many well wishers how I honestly just felt
warmed up and trained for this life of mine. That I'm finally
getting the hang of this game. I think that's because I really

only started paying attention to how to do it a few years ago. Learning how to be ME in the world this way, not just what looked right or was expected of someone with my opportunities. I completely love it. I know my purpose now, clearly and calmly. Someone in a class I was listening to today said the everyone has the same purpose in life, to be ourselves. The rest was just things we did or ways we helped at certain times. I like that. Sorry if any of you told me this ages ago! I remain a slow learner in these things. It's why I feel so very lucky to have been given the time to figure it out. I hope I have lots more to practise it. I hope you do too.

On your envelopes this month I tried something new too! Inspired by all the printmaker artists I'm surrounded with at the gallery I thought I would try to do some printing with leaves on your envelopes. I used strawberry, a tip of some bracken and a teeny tiny oak leaf. Some are better than others, but the experiment was joyful just like most things that leave your fingers stained.

The Local Grapevine

I have had the most fun couple of days distributing free grape plants. Lovely Anton, who used to look after us on the estate, messaged me last week saying he knew of some free grapes going and if I wanted a few I should call his friend. So I did. I was immediately dropped into this amazing story where the son of a Russian Oligarch (who happens to be one of Vladimir Putin's best buddies from KGB days) has bought an estate on the Cowal Penninsula. It's a lovely spot at the end of Loch Striven and looks across the East Kyle to the island of Bute. This fellow has done the research and is planting a vineyard on the slopes of the estate. He's imported 8000 or so vines from Germany of varieties that are expected to handle our climate and make nice wine or eating grapes. They finished their project and about 650 plants were languishing in the game larder of Anton's pal. It's almost hunting season and this fellow needed to get them out of the fridge! They'd tried to sell them, but just didn't know anyone who could absorb them. That's where we come in. So I drove over there on Tuesday for a little adventure. Met the loveliest couple and got a glimpse at the big project. Wow. It felt quite visionary and I love when people bet on themselves in that way. (Obviously I prefer when the money to do so hasn't been looted from the Russian people to do it).

So when confronted with a fridge full of plants I got excited and brought 125 home! I don't own my own land or you know I would have immediately entered the wine growing business despite my last name. But I knew that so many people would love to have even one grape vine in their poly tunnels or glasshouses here like I have. So I brought them home and activated

The experimental grape estate on Loch Striven.

the local grapevine. (I'm proud of what I did there). In a few years there will hopefully be so many people in this area eating grapes and making their own wine! We're giving them out at a pace and I have been introduced to one lovely couple who might take the punt on a couple hundred and plant the lot next spring! Really, really fun to play grape Robin Hood. I've of course planted a couple in pots myself and will guerrilla plant some around the walled garden and orchard. I often marvel at those who left all the trees and bushes for me and it will be wonderful to think that I've added something long term to the mix. An unexpected delight that hopefully benefits many.

View from my camping spot on Barra.

An Adventure in the Hebrides

I'd been feeling restless at the end of July. Like old me, itchy feet to be somewhere else. I was craving different sights and smells and just a break up to my, lovely, routine. It was kind of exciting to feel that way again honestly. My friends sailing with Golago had gotten stuck in Stornaway on the Isle of Lewis in the Outer Hebrides while they did engine repairs. I had been dreaming at stopping at an internet friend's cafe on the island of Harris, the weather was great and I wondered if car camping was something you should really do in your 40s, so I figured why not? I planned myself a circular route (my favourite kind) that took me from Oban (just a couple of hours away) by sea to the southern most island of the Outer Hebrides called Barra. And from there I would ferry ever northwards through the Uists and Benbecula and then up to Harris and Lewis. I would take a late ferry to Ullapool from there and begin about a five hour drive home.

The plan was to sleep in my car—which I can make a very good single bed in and the rest of the space is for Alfred who also makes a great heater. I researched like crazy to find an event shelter kind of tent that I could put up around the

Morning coffee on a stormy day.

back of the car to make a waterproof living/cooking space to make it all work. The only thing that didn't work out was some very high winds on the Hebrides so I only put my tent up on one night on Harris. It was lovely though. It rained that next morning and it was brilliant to sit in my lawn chair with my coffee and breakfast and not worry about anything.

The Outer Hebrides (or The Western Isles as you may have heard them called) are spectacular places filled with sandy beaches and turquoise water. Gaelic is still spoken regularly and not just in a way to preserve the language. The accent is filled with lilts and feels like Irish and Welsh have married into what you expect from a rural Scottish sound. It's wonderful. The last night

The walk just beyond the must visit Temple Cafe on Harris.

of camping on Harris someone had climbed up into the hills above the beach and was yodelling, proper yodelling and calling. It was amazing. But the trip is best showcased in photos so I'll let them do that.

At Home

My wonderful neighbours kept the plants going while I was gone and it was a pleasure to get home to their tending again. The tomatoes that have made it past the blight (mostly cherry varieties) are doing wonderful and there's enough to feed me.

My friend Becky who is a residential cook at some highland estate properties had come to stay between jobs and she used everything I could pick her each day to treat me like a complete queen. The day she left I ate popcorn and toast, I'm not sure she'll forgive me. But it was a perfect re-entry into the world with all it's scary and difficult things. We took it all in, took action where we could and then took care of ourselves. I know I say this all the time but we must know how to be resilient in order to process and act as we would wish in these stunningly difficult times. In order to advocate for refugees and climate action we must also be well and rested. It's ok not to watch the news every day multiple times a day. It's ok to tag out so you can come back to us strong and hopeful. And that might take longer than you think. Especially if you've been at this world thing for a while. No one was interested in you getting rest, just you getting "it" done.

The cottage has been sleeping in mists most nights right now. We're having a little pattern of a warm afternoon, stunning sunset, and then mists visibly gathering as the sun goes. It's completely stunning and sees me running outside in my socks at least twice to try and get a photo. First when the sunset is just too stunning and then again when the mist, coloured by the pink or orange air of sunset starts to build and huff from the hollows until it wraps around everything. The liquid air is cool and you think it's the end of the heat, but the cool still mornings are burned away and the cycle starts again.

The seals are back in number in the bay and I've missed them so. I've got a small pair of binoculars now and it's added so much to my morning walks when it comes to the seals sleeping on their islands and all the little water birds that aren't close enough to identify with the naked eye.

The butterflies have finally arrived in full force and I have spent delicious amounts of time watching them on the flowers.

Much love,

Susie
xx

"What ails you?"
- The wise knight with a different way who asked the Fisher King what was needed instead of busying about with ideas of quests and dramatic acts.
The balance and health of the world was restored.

SEPTEMBER 2021

The Gardeners Cottage
Argyll's Secret Coast
Scotland, UK

September 29, 2021

Dearest friend,

I am never so aware and humbled by the magic in-

The fennel growing outside my living room window providing both privacy and flavour to be!

volved in creation of any sort—you might call it inspiration, flow, downloads, or vision—then when I try to make it come at my bidding! (Note the date of this month's letter). Every now and again I dismiss all the whispers and ideas as they come. The gifts dropped into my consciousness of a way to tell a story or translate a feeling. I don't capture them when they are streaming. I assume there will be another day, there will be more, that there is an infinite supply and my timings are the master here. But it sure isn't. And when it's the time I decree as appropriate I'm humbly left unable even to approach a keyboard let alone pull something good from it. And I feel unconvinced that I may never be able to call it down to me again. It's so uncomfortable.

I think: this time I will learn the lesson. But I won't. Not entirely.

I believe in the infinite possibility of so many things, but I also know from nature that everything isn't always available all the time. You can stand amidst a thousand apple trees, but if it is not autumn you cannot eat. I wonder how hard we have worked to build entire systems so humans did not have to face the feeling of uncertainty in 'not now' or 'not yet'? This current season of harvest around the grounds of the estate—the pears, plums, apples, blackberries, tomatoes finishing, seed collection—has made me think about my relationship to opportunity and learning how to do something new. And my own creative projects and the rest of the global human world is really making me consider my relationship with uncertainty.

I read a quote this month from Dr. Michael Bloomfield, a creativity expert and researcher:

> "If you look upon uncertainty as an opportunity for discovery of novel things or ways of looking at things, as a driver of randomised divergence, you can re-frame uncertainty as a positive and construct form of fuel for creativity."

For me the balance is provided by nature's teachings in this. That there is a cycle that moves through opportunity and uncertainty and back again. As part of nature we face uncertainty all the time, we can't avoid it. It has led to us creating the most extraordinary things in order to take advantage of the opportunities also provided. But every opportunity is not perpetual.

When we attempted to make all opportunity always available we believed we had removed ourselves from the cycle. But we didn't. We just broke our right relationship to it. And the rest of nature has been out there dealing with the uncertainty of what we have done. We're just getting to see the answers to our wrong belief that we were sovereign here in our creation of climate change.

And yet, nature (including us) is extraordinary and there are often unacknowledged opportunities completely surrounding us. The magic moves, but it doesn't disappear. I can see it in the way that food gardening is having a resurgence. Completely wonderful for changing food systems and insecurity AND welcoming our human selves back into relationship with the cycles of uncertainty and opportunity.

Harvest

So much is going on each day it's been hard to keep up. The beginning of the month was still high summer. Hot sunny days, foods ripening fast. It felt like summer would go on forever. But the first trees started to change their leaves and the first formation of geese passed towards the south. Autumn has always

Wild hazel nuts (or cobnuts) waiting to have their husks removed.

been my favourite season. It's funny because there is so much change within it—maybe I like change more than I think!

I've been so busy trying to put more fruits and preserves away. It started with tomatoes. My neighbour Sophie is the finest grower of tomatoes I know. Her gluts are legendary! I spent many hours roasting tray after tray of them in the oven with olive oil, garlic, rosemary and thyme. I didn't quite have the energy to commit to making specific things, so I made the building blocks of future things and that felt wonderful.

Beautiful hydrangeas with a cheeky Alfred photobomb I just noticed.

The pears have had a wonderful year. They are huge and completely gorgeous. Pears need to be picked from the tree to finish ripening otherwise they will simply rot from the inside out. You pick them from the trees with one quick test. If you lift the pear upwards above its branch if it snaps off it's time! If if doesn't you leave it a bit longer. There are many pears slowly coming to ripeness in the kitchen and I will definitely be full of pear processing next month.

The apples are also coming ripe now. I have gotten a little obsessive with dehydrating apple slices. They also taste like candy and get consumed by the handful so they are disappearing quickly too. I'm doing some now for my neighbours from our communal apple stash too. I'm sure I'll be bored of them eventually, but not just yet!

Blackberries and hazel nuts are the wild story of the moment. The hazelnuts aren't nearly as prolific as last year, but I have a lovely stash to make a treat or two. When I pick the hazels I only pick from my feet so that everything above my reach (usually a lot) is left for the rest of the creatures. The blackberries (brambles) are a complete joy. I had a really fun experiment this summer where in the early part of the season in the walled garden I started to make topiary structures out of the bramble vines. I thought it might be a fun way to retain the fruit, but also control the spread of the vines a little. What I learned from this was that it actually concentrated all the berry growth

Pears and blackberries waiting to be made into something delicious.

in convenient locations! I basically have three small stops to fill up a colander every couple of days. The runners from those spots also don't seem to bear any of the fruits. So next year I will take the work a little more seriously and see if I can duplicate it again and in an even more pleasing manner! I'm thinking sweet pea towers and blackberry arches! (I'm nuts I know).

A family of ravens have also forayed into the lower grounds of the estate and caused quite an excitement amongst the crows and buzzards. The ravens were incredibly precise about the way they moved in and moved off the other birds. They spoke to each other constantly and I loved the low rumbles of sound that is only theirs. They of course eluded excellent photography with my phone.

Your envelope this month attempts to showcase the other most talked about animal on the estate: the elusive otter. My neighbour Effie had a completely wonderful visit from one who had not noticed her presence on one of the further beaches (whale bone beach if you remember). Our other neighbour Mick remains unlucky with a sighting and is completely desperate to enjoy one. So we have much enjoyment about the trickster otters and who they reveal themselves to around here. I so wanted to capture the otter artistically for you. I tried at least six different sketches and perspectives and I was a complete failure!!! So I made this very playful silhouette for you until one deigns to visit completely.

Part of my sunflower harvest.

A little tidbit of otter folklore for you where otters were often characterised as a friendly and helpful creature. In Scotland there are tales of 'Otter Kings' who were accompanied by seven black otters. When captured, these beasts would grant any wish in exchange for their freedom. But their skins were also prized for their ability to render a warrior invincible, and were thought to provide protection against drowning. Luckily, the Otter Kings were hard to kill, their only vulnerable point being a small point below their chin. In the Irish story The Voyage of Maelduin, otters on the Island of Otter bring the sailors salmon to eat, and the Voyage of Brendan tells of how an otter performed this service for a hermit, even collecting firewood for him! St. Cuthbert is the patron saint of otters, and after standing waist-deep in the North Sea during his nightly prayer vigils, two otters would come and warm his feet with their breath and dry them with their fur.

A Smaller, Slower World

I'm not sure if I've written to you much about my knee injury this year. Starting in January and with a big re-injury in April that hasn't recovered I've had a painful summer. The NHS (our national health service) is really struggling to respond to normal things like this at the moment (please get vaccinated if you haven't already) and I've been waiting since the beginning of August to have an X-ray read! What this has meant is that my world has been a little smaller this summer. Where normally my walks in the warmth of summer range further and I explore more places I have been slowed down and contracted. I desperately wish for it to be better, but I haven't missed the irony in being asked by my body at this time to go even slower and get even more intimate with landscape I traverse every day. I'm sure we'll get there eventually, but the experience has amplified my empathy for those of you who have always been dealing with chronic pain and mobility issues. My inability to climb hills and carry loads has changed the way I'm relating to nature from a physical perspective, but it hasn't changed the power of the connection that's possible.

A Gallery Show

I have been convinced by my very wonderful friend and the owner of Tighnabruaich Gallery to do a display of my book in the Gallery before Christmas! So my little book, some note-cards, and some blown up images from my photography will be available to purchase. Of course part of me is petrified. Another part didn't want to do it because I didn't want the horrible old estate manager to be able to thumb through my book! Hahahah, but as usual I sat and had a little chat with myself and remembered that I am so proud of what has been done, what we did together! I am not embarrassed by how much I love this landscape and what I know and also how I'm learning as I go. I might be afraid to be known so intimately by those that surround me, but I can live with that more than not saying yes to the opportunities (that word again) that are available to me right now. So I will prepare for that these next few weeks and report back! (I am writing this in the gallery right now and a lovely local woman came in and had much praise for this project and my Instagram work so that's very funny. Ok, Ok universe I hear you it's a good thing.)

Much love,
Susie
Xx

OCTOBER 2021

The Gardeners Cottage
Argyll's Secret Coast
Scotland, UK

October 24, 2021

Dear Friends,

A dolphin on The Clyde. Full story inside.

October, October! Already!
And already almost ended. Does anyone else feel like Time itself
has changed in the last two years? That even that doesn't move
in the way I anticipate anymore?

And so many people I know and love (including myself) have
had a pretty intense month this month. Many big highs, intense
lows, boundary settings, physical things to deal with, the afore-
mentioned rapid and yet slippery and slow time. Emotions have
been deep and swift and incapable of being ignored or stuffed
down. Pretty much like everything else. The time for that
coping behaviour even pretending to work in the short term
seems to be over everywhere.

So if time has been playing with you and it has felt like A
LOT I just want you to know that you are not alone. Accept this
letter as a long hug from someone who cares about you and
wants you to thrive and receive what you need no matter what
shape your battered heart might be in right now. (And if you're
human your heart has had a battering at some point).

As things piled on this month and harms were done to me
and by me, as always here, I retreated to nature for guidance

and peace. I was sitting on the white quartz of the one I call Secret Beach and I was thinking about reparations. Reparations is a word we use a lot right now as we face the true histories of our nation and systems building. It means the action of making amends for a wrong one has done.

And I thought about how what anti-racist activists like the brilliant Nova Reid (her book The Good Ally is out now) are asking us to understand first is so important. The idea that good people can do harm. That the two aren't exclusive. It's inevitable not to do harm to others (which doesn't mean you don't try to avoid doing it or take it very seriously when it happens). Somewhere in the system building the story was created that if we were "good" we couldn't do harm, so therefore we were completely unable to hear that harm had been done because then we would be "bad"— and no one wants to be bad. So through gaslighting, ignoring, apologies that aren't apologies, etc so many harms get even bigger because we've mostly been unable to hold our sometimes harmful impacts on each other as something that can live beside our goodness. It's like what Brene Brown writes about the difference between shame and guilt. Shame is: I am bad. Guilt is: I did something bad. One can be answered. Reparations are the natural answer to doing something bad.

And what if one of the answers to all this mess that our world is in right now was making reparations become our deepest joy? What if understanding that we do harm all the time becomes something we accept about ourselves because we are human and all a bit broken and battered and systematised to extract and that shows sometimes in how we act to each other or the skills we have or lack for dealing with each other. What if every apology and amends opportunity was our joy? A cauterised wrong in a planet bleeding to death in individual and systemic hurt. And I don't mean glossing over the pain of understanding you caused harm to another or the discomfort of seeing a version of yourself you might wish was different. But knowing that when you go into that discomfort and pain and guilt with sincerity and humility that you are in fact being the best version of yourself? It's not an opportunity you want, but when you find yourself in one you get to take the event as a moment to find your best self again and proceed from there.

How much easier would the systemic reparations that are due to our planet, the impacts of colonialism, victims of slavery and their descendants, First Nations people, etc be to understand and implement if we knew how to give them personally? If we imagined our "best-self" nations and institutions too. I just wonder and I'm going to try and ask this of myself.

Also I have just rewatched the entirety of the tv show *The Good Place*, so I might be a bit philosophical this month. Again.

Networks

One of the great joys this month was painting your envelopes! It was such happy work and for the first time in ages (or at all) I felt like I was actually working with the water colour paint like it's meant to used. Normally it takes me many days to get through all the envelopes, but this delightful fungi friend arrived easily and quickly. Another layer of joy!

The entire month has been about mushrooms. Once the moisture returned they have been popping up proudly in the thousands! I've filled the letter with pictures of so many species I have found in the woods around the estate. They are so incredibly beautiful and it's mesmerising to start looking at them closely and realising what you don't know. The only ones we ate have been the Chanterelles which I have found in a couple of locations now. Neither of which is where I expected them, a perfect demonstration of how much there is to learn about mushrooms!!!

Getting curious about mushrooms is like finding a whole new language/solar system in which I am a complete foreigner. I bought a beautiful book of all the mushrooms of the UK and most of Europe. But it's hard to work backwards from. I need to learn all the mushroom parts and train my eye to see the differences that are there... just not yet for me!

But like everything nature had such a lesson for me this month in what I noticed and of course it was about networks. Mushrooms are the fruit of the invisible and healthy mycelium network in the soil. This is the internet of all things. I always think it's wonderful that we basically made our own mycelium network because we forgot how to be plugged in to the real one. We share knowledge about how to replug in on it. That gives me joy to hold on to when the information system gets misused for being horrible to each other.

And it's so important to remember that because we don't see it or understand how it is happening doesn't mean it isn't! We understand so very little about our planet yet. Trees care for each other through it. Disease gets responded to. Bugs and worms and minerals all interacting to make the best environment possible. We can do our bit, but it will never be as good as what the more than human world already knows how to do.

Ancestors and Dolphins

I did something this week that I have been wanting to do for a while. After I moved here I learned that our (a few of my wonderful cousins get these letters too) great grand father sailed to Canada (ensuring my existence) from Greenock where I regularly embark on the ferry. On the 4th of April, 1925 in 3rd class John Allen boarded the SS Canada, his passage paid as an Empire Settlement Scheme, from The Tail of The Bank dock in Greenock. He was all alone. We don't know much about him besides the fact that he did harm to my Grandmother when she eventually was forced to join him after her grandparents died. His mother is listed here as next of kin. He is called a farm worker here and is supposed to get assigned from the Settlement department upon arrival in Saskatoon, Saskatchewan. Where coincidently I went to University. I don't know if he ever made it to Saskatoon. All I have ever known of the story is in Ontario. From Halifax, where he disembarked to Saskatoon is over 3000 km and that's room for a lot of decision making.

My Great-Grandfather's immigration record to Canada from Scotland in 1925.

He was 23 years old. Probably never expecting to go home again. And I think of him every time I am riding over the Clyde and looking out towards the sea. All the disused and repurposed docks at Greenock where hundreds of thousands like him were expelled from their homes in service of empire and opportunity while the lands here were stripped further of its people. Colonialism does violence on its foot soldiers as much as war.

So yesterday while I was waiting for car repairs, I jumped on the ferry to Gourock to amuse myself. While having a lovely breakfast overlooking The Clyde I remembered John. I went and looked up the spot he left from. A walk down the shore now all bicycle paths and playgrounds for local residents and I found the perfect view of the red buoy that marked the course of the boats out of Tail of the Bank.

And I stood there leaning on the metal railing. It was sunny and warm. I let my shadow be cast on the Clyde and I imaged myself back in time and wanted him to feel me there waving him away, caring about him and standing and watching until he was out of sight when there likely wasn't anyone who did.

And when I felt finished I went and sat on a swing in the playground. And just as I got comfortable in the motion, feeling young and happy, I saw something on the water. A pod of dolphins surfaced and started feeding just off shore. I laughed out loud. I ran back to the rail and I stopped a young woman with her daughter so they could see. She turned out to be a very new immigrant here from Hong Kong, alone with her baby daughter waiting for her husband to join them.

Dolphins mean a lot to me. They have always arrived for me in moments of deep feeling. When I thought they had swum beyond me I began walking back to the ferry. I realised exactly why I was called there that day and I had done it and it had been welcomed. When I got to the ferry the dolphins were literally there waiting! They were swimming around the boat, showing themselves and slapping their tails, and just generally delighting us all. Pure magic.

Still The Harvest Goes On!

With the return of the rain the mushrooms weren't the only ones having their moment. October was definitely about getting some apples processed. I have been dehydrating them by the load, sharing with neighbours and also just eating them as snacks already because they are delicious! I've put some apple

cider in the freezer for winter cheer at hand. And I've made a few batches of Apple Butter. If you haven't encountered apple butter it isn't butter, but like a really condensed apple sauce that you can use as a spread. I am planning it for yogurt and porridge additions once the fresh fruit has stopped coming. I've been making mine in the slow cooker (thanks Anna!) and it makes the house smell gorgeous.

A medlar fruit.

I've been trying to finish processing (or just eat) the pears as they ripen too. The pears have been ridiculously tasty. On one of my walks with visiting friends I came across a sweet chestnut tree covered in nuts to be! I hope I manage to get a few to try and roast on my own. I have a delicious recipe for chestnut, sage and onion bread that I adore and wouldn't it be fab to make with ingredients all from home?

I have finally achieved my first Medlar harvest! I was so excited about them when I moved here and then there were the difficulties with the former estate manager and I didn't get to harvest. Last year they flowered before the pollinators arrived and there were no fruit. But this year they were happy and huge! Medlars are another one of those fruits that have been pushed out of our western consciousness because of the time they take to process. You need to let them blet or rot a bit before you use them. This often happens naturally on the tree after a frost. So after our first little frost I collected them in. I've shared half of them with my friend Amanda (who runs that gorgeous cafe on the island of Harris) who knows everything and will share what she decides to do. I will then attempt to copy her. Hahaha. I will report back.

Those of you who follow me on social media know that Alfred has hurt his back leg and is on strict rest. It makes for a different experience not to head out with him every morning on an adventure. Hopefully by the time I write  you next he'll be bouncing about as himself again. I'm off to Canada for the longest overdue visit to family so it will be an adventure in humanity I think a bit this month ahead!

Much love,
Susie xx

"Earth is... so kind... just tickle her... and she laughs with a harvest."
—Douglas William Jerrold

NOVEMBER 2021

The Gardeners Cottage
Argyll's Secret Coast
Scotland, UK

December 3, 2021

Dear Friend,

It's not often a letter of
November starts in December,
but that's life at The Gardeners Cottage this month. Best of
intentions often don't meet
reality straight on, in so many
ways, and I ran out of the head
start I had given myself last
month quite quickly before the end of the month!

Sunlight on the water over Greenland. I
have been flying this route for over a
decade and this used to be all ice,
especially in November. Another
climate heartbreak and the irony of
being in an airplane while I see it is not
lost on me.

In November I was so incredibly lucky to get to return to
Canada to see my family in Saskatchewan and some beloved
friends (but definitely not all) in Alberta. I didn't know how
much I needed that. How much the pandemic and the absence
of the possibility of time with them had cost me. It was a lot. A
trip home had never been more welcome or even completely,
joyfully dwelt in. I didn't hurry and spent wonderful, thoughtful time with everyone. It was more conversation and card
games, baby cuddling, meals shared and prepared, and basically
loving each other in each other's physical presence. We
celebrated missed everythings, new babies and engagements
and new apartments and kitchen renovations and early Christmas decorating! Even with all the swabs up nose—as I took

Lateral Flow tests each day to make sure I wasn't carrying COVID between locations—it felt so very good.

Returning home to winter light.

As I returned home to news of the new Omicron variant and tighter travel restrictions returning I felt lucky for the window of time I managed to squeeze through. The travel itself was very disconcerting at first. Packed into a plane filled with people when I hadn't been in more than a not-very-crowded restaurant in two years took some inner dialogue calming! I had to stop recalculating my risk in each moment and just do the things I could do—wear my mask, wash my hands, don't touch my darn face (so hard!), and take my tests every day and deal with the results if I had to. It was hard to trust my fellow humans to do the same! But with even a few conversations and overhearing others what I quickly realised that the plane was filled with people like me. On their way or returning from seeing long-absent loved ones. The pleasure of meeting kind strangers sharing a journey was something I had forgotten in these last two years of retreat. And it is something I had always quite loved about the world. So I am deeply grateful for all of it.

Being in western Canada also made me even more aware of how unwild it actually is here on these islands of Britain. An ecosystem with humanity as the only apex predator remains a park requiring constant intervention. Reading the local newspapers in Canmore, Alberta discussing living with bears, bobcats and kits in a friend's Calgary back alley, my sister not being able to walk a few blocks to work in the early mornings because of the potential of cougars in town, seeing big healthy coyotes and hearing their songs from within the city... it made me sad for the extent of what has been done here, what is gone. That even the return of the sea eagle was almost denied because it might eat lambs (instead of being required to invest and protect our livestock like we would have before). The lynx, the bear, the wolf... all eradicated from this place where they used to thrive too. I know many of you who receive this letter live in places with these other creatures still live. I beg of you to treasure that. Participate in your community treasuring that and dealing with some losses and risk instead of eradicating them if you can. It can happen there too. Find those organisations and report back to me! I'd truly love to know what it might look like where you live.

Archeology

What I most wanted to write about this month is archeology —"the study of human activity through the recovery and analysis of material culture. The archeological record consists of things like artefacts, architecture, biofacts, sites, cultural landscapes." There is so much archeology discovered and yet undiscovered in this part of Scotland. Standing stones and cairns and iron age forts. Pottery and jewellery and weaponry and tools. Carved stones for ritual or direction or feel free to make it up!

I got to thinking also about the making of archeology, the things of daily life that are accidentally preserved and how my dropped pen might be the only thing anyone has to make up the whole story of my life and how I lived it. How it's only the things we even know HOW to look for that get found. I have

often written about all the sites of interest I keep finding here on the estate at Ardmarnoch. Things in the landscape that feel intentional not accidental (if geology is accidental). The cuts in the rock always on the way to a view point like the one pictured. Fallen stones that look like more standing stones and cairns that aren't mapped.

A passageway in the landscape near Whale Bone Beach with an interesting cut into the rock face.

Is the study of archeology just another way we as humans try to be known? To know if we map the ancestors' lives perhaps someday our own will be known and valued beyond the moment too?

Before I went away I found myself watching all these incredible online talks from Archeology Scotland and the Kilmartin Museum. I'm so fascinated with the rock markings and what they know and don't know about what they mean. I tried to recreate some on our envelopes this month. One of the talks I attended is how they were using statistics now to evaluate the position of all the known sites and how that is led to a much more informative pattern than they've had before. And giving credence to the theory that they might be used as directional and informational signage.

The view of the Iron Age hilltop fort I look at every day. It's the grouping of trees on top of the hill at the left side of the photo.

As the bracken pulls back with winter and dies away all those interesting parts of the landscape call out to me again to notice them. The surely cairns and bases to structures my eyes pick out of the landscape now whether for real or for a story I'm creating about this place. I have mapped many of the sites on What3Words, but winter always brings with it the desire to do and know more about it.

I think a lot about why so much of this particular archaeology still exists in Scotland and it's of course because of the clearing from the countryside of the people. The wealthy used the cairn stones to build their stone walls. Sheep and wildlife don't bother too much with ruins except to eat around them and use them for protection and scratching. The stories they contain are only valuable to some. And having been home to western Canada it made me think about the archaeology we ploughed through or didn't mark because it didn't look like a valuable story to us, fire circles and medicine wheels in the prairie, but perhaps it was a camp that had been used for 10,000 years and the location was full of stories about that landscape too. As always I'm just so grateful for the opportunity to dream about these things.

Darkness

It's 4:15pm as I write on and darkness has already dropped. There is a purple-inky pink to the clouds in the west where the last of the light is reflecting high in the sky only. 16 days until solstice an Instagram friend wrote today. 16 more days until we start the climb back out of the darkness. No wonder the ancestors made monuments about these moments. How different their winters must have been. How important the promise that light always returns, that the sun goes on its quest to the south but always, always returns.

Here it's the time for star walks at 6pm and enjoying as much of the moon as it wants to give us. In Scotland the cloudy days of dark can be hardest, where the limited light there could be is filtered through thick, low cloud. It's why Christmas decorations make so much sense and candles are cheerful! Some years I mind and some years I don't. This seems to be one of the latter. I do think my ability to navigate this time of year has a lot to do with how I have designed my life and having the room most of the time for just surrendering to a 4 o'clock completion. Last spring as the light returned I actually had a hard time settling back into extended opportunities for productivity! I try to listen to my body as much as I can. I try to sit with the sun on my face when it's possible and not hurry passed it like there are more urgent things to do. I feel like I want to really surrender to the darkness this year and then mark solstice a little more intentionally than just a whispered "thank god" as I look at the sunset times expanding again, minute by minute on the BBC weather app.

Bird Watching Season

The winter cold has brought back bird feeding and watching season. The delights outside my desk window are enough to keep anyone attempting to work. My joy in them all is so real. It's splendid to be a part of their world. They set off all the bird notifications when I go out to fill the feeders and soon everyone descends and takes their turns, or not, at the suet or seeds. My little robins have separated for their winter break, one here at the front of the house with most of the others, and the other inside the walled garden again.

My little brave one is still about, although its been pushed further out by the return of the parent. It's funny to watch the parent try and chase it further off from the meal worms I bring each day. I try to settle the parent at the prime location and then go for the baby separately. I know it's them because they are fearless! Where the parents have gotten all shy after a summer of not coming to hand, little one flies right on and gets what they need. They follow Alfred about like maybe he's the key to the food? It's really funny to watch. I'm not sure what will happen come spring. Will my little one go off and make a family of their own? Will they go find a partner and bring it back close? Will they bring their babies to me the way their father did? It's incredibly lovely to think about my multi-generational relationship with the robins of the estate.

And just a final note to let you know that his lordship Alfred is doing so much better! All four legs are back in use although still tenderly. We are at the point of recovery where I am walking him on lead because I don't want him to run too much and hurt himself again before the healing is done. He takes it all with his good will and cheerful demeanour despite clearly not understanding what has gotten into me!

"One of the most interesting parts is the detective element. Archaeology is like a jigsaw puzzle, except that you can't cheat and look at the box, and not all the pieces are there."
—Stephen Dean, 2013

Much love,
Susie xx

DECEMBER 2021

The Gardeners Cottage
Argyll's Secret Coast
Scotland, UK

December 31, 2021

Dearest friends,

December is such a strange
month in this project. The
physical letter subscribers all
get a holiday card, this year one from a wild life trust so not
bespoke. So I thought instead of just duplicating that I would
write you, my wonderful digitally based friends a short note of
gratitude on this final day of the year.

I find New Year's strange. I have had one truly joyous
version of it back in the 2000's with my friend Cecilia in Seattle.
We went out for Thai and then went Bollywood dancing until
we fell out of the club at midnight, drenched in sweat and joy,
to watch the fireworks light up the Space Needle. It was
completely wonderful and I've yet to see it's likes again.

What I do love about New Year's is the concept of Auld Lang
Syne—the missing and remembering of distant friends. If ever
there was a series of years that made this an important pause,
this is it. And although so many of us have lost people we love
and admire this year, we've also had to be distant from so many
because of the pandemic. As someone who takes a lot of
pleasure in time by myself I am really starting to feel this one.
So I send a lot of love to you if it is you too.

Mostly this year I've been thinking about continuing to shed and questioning why I'm doing things or wanting things. Making sure I'm not doing or longing for solutions based on trauma response to my own life experience or the systems still ruling our fragile world. Mostly what I'm trying to say is that it is all so complicated, unpredictable, and quite hard at the moment for so many. And doing my best is more than enough. We won't build a new kind of world from our pain. That's the old song and it doesn't serve us to let it be sung anymore.

So what do I do to bring myself ease and joy and hope despite feeling small and not enough? I feed the little robins. I make their winter a little more gentle. I remember that my worthiness isn't conditional and I try and help you remember that too. My wish for 2022 is that we do.

Happy New Year and much love,

Susie
xx

Wintery scenes above Black Harbour.

JANUARY 2022

The Gardeners Cottage
Argyll's Secret Coast
Scotland, UK

January 24, 2021

Greetings my dear friends!

I thought each of you
might enjoy starting the year
with your very own robin in
your hand. I'm so pleased with

**A magnolia blossom on the tree today.
Spring is coming early.**

this month's envelopes. They are based on photos of my actual
little friend who gives me so much joy each time it lands in my
hand. If you get even a dollop of that joy from these envelopes I
will consider my year well started.

They say the island of Arran is like all of Scotland in miniature—it has the highmountains and the coastlines with little
islands around it and beautiful glens and lochs all within its
90km (about 55 mile) circumference. I feel like January has
been a year in miniature!

It's been filled with accomplishments and fallowness. Lots of
planning and creation. And as always, more learning. I don't
often hit January running, but this year after having a December focused on care of self and recovery, and basically completely skipping the obligations of Christmas, I actually
emerged on schedule with the modern calendar year. One of
the historical wormholes I keep going down in regards to the
Age of the Saints here on the west coast of

The air has been going pink in the evening a lot this month as the cloud cover holds the sunset light low and diffused.

Scotland is how they held out on the changes to the calendar until well into the 9th Century. I get that resistance to scheduling, but more on history in a bit.

The weather has been incredibly mild and I imagine even though we've not come to the traditional markers of its early arrival, that for us here, spring is indeed coming in quickly. The temperatures have been very warm for January and there are blooms or buds formed in unexpected places.

The pheasant season ends in one more week and walking here on the estate really hits the best time of the year. It might be rainy or cold, but the bracken is dead and the deer paths clear, and there are no pens full of birds to avoid. That means longer walks into quieter places and it is my absolute favourite time to explore the landscape of the estate more intimately.

Garden Things

I have been busy pruning roses and preparing the outside beds. I finally got a good tidy done in the glasshouse this week knowing that things start to move quickly soon with the return of the light. I have finally got a bit of a rhythm for planting. Focusing first on flowers then moving on to veg which might need more warmth.

But that being said I ate my first ever January tomatoes this month! (Those of you who follow me on Instagram will already know this because it was not something I could keep to myself until I wrote!) I had planted the tomato plants in late July and these particular fruits were formed before the real dark and cold. They just slowly slowly came to

ripeness. There are more on the bushes and I am very interested to see what will happen now as the light returns. Will I have a steady source of tomatoes by March? Is the trick getting the plants to overwinter so that just like my autumn planted ranunculus and sweet peas they are poised to take immediate advantage of the spring light? Light which of course is equivalent to autumn light when they are still growing.

Questions to be answered with time. I have kept the tomatoes on a bottom heated surface, but in the glasshouse all winter. I only covered them a few days and have been cutting off any really dead bits or blossoms that dried without fruiting. I write so much detail because I want to remember and I want to challenge us all to keep working on extending the period of time in the year which we feed ourselves. Every little bit of food that doesn't come on a truck or wrapped in plastic is a successful rebellion these days. I saw a fellow who is homesteading in Alaska with ripe cherry tomatoes on his kitchen windowsill in December and thought I could be trying a bit harder!

I managed to complete the biggest prune and tidy I've ever done of the grape vine in the glasshouse. I took back all the long shoots that were either attempting to escape the roof or extend the vine's dominion to more of the glasshouse. In summer when the leaves are full the shade is welcome to some of the plants (and me), but the heat lovers like the tomatoes and cucumbers have to grow on the other side. And the lack of light really impacted the veg I tried on the (turned off) propagating table last year. We are back to a nice, hopefully dappled lattice structure. And with less miles of vine to feed I am also hoping for fewer and bigger fruit and maybe this will be the year I beat the wasps to it!

The Night Sky

The full moon above the cottage.

I have not been sleeping at all normally this month despite the busy-ness of the days. I am normally a very good sleeper even though I am often a lucid dreaming sort. (The kind where you are consciously participating while they are happening.). But deep sleep has not been a gift of January. I have had many nights this month cursing the brightness of the moonlight and envious of Alfred's snoring while I am still so very awake. The skies have been very clear though and it has had me outside staring at stars again. I don't know if it's all the historical learning I've been doing the past couple of months combined that I was recently home in Canada, but I started wondering about how the old sailors or travellers must have felt when they looked at the sky far from home. Do they look at the night horizon and long for the stars to be in the right place to them? If we navigated by the stars surely there must have been a moment, when the stars were in a particular part of the sky that felt like home? I wonder if it's deep in our DNA to look for them.

The first constellations I ever learned were the Big Dipper and Orion. The Big Dipper has so many names called The Plough here and in other places: the wagon, the pot, the caribou, and part of the Big Bear. It is a creature of the north too, always there to help you find true north and make your way around.

But Orion is the one who makes me long for stars to be in their "home" spot for me. He is always found too far south here for where I expect him and we even lose him for a bit in summer.

I long for him then.

I remember being in Zimbabwe once and seeing him in the north sky, upside down, and I knew I was indeed far from home. I also remember my delight at finally seeing The Southern Cross on a trip to Australia and the way that thrilled me to be on such an adventure. Anyway, while I am awake long into the night I sit and think of all the early seafaring folks whether in hide boats or ships and how they might have longed for the stars to be in a particular spot for them just as I do.

I worry about everyone who can't see the stars at all anymore. Do they feel lost?

The Age of the Vikings

I enjoyed another fine archeological talk from The Kilmartin Museum online. This month it was about evidence of the Vikings in Argyll. Interestingly enough there isn't that much once you come off the islands. And what there is usually comes later and shows a combination of beliefs. Evidence like Christian crosses with runes written on the edges and the repurposing of things like decoration from illuminated manuscripts as jewellery. But as always there is this big emptiness of evidence when it comes to our side of Loch Fyne. I find that hole fascinating! I asked the question this time about why there was such a lack of knowledge or evidence and one of the theories is that the peoples in this spot did not participate in the Viking economy that was happening around them. So they weren't in possession of its treasures like silver etc, to bury with them. Another was simply no one has really looked. But the vikings were all around including finds on Bute and the little island of Inchmarnock (perhaps the site of the monastery of St Marnoch with its unknown ties to the land here—Ardmarnoch). So mysteries of the past keep calling!

You can check out any of the talks on the Kilmartin Museum's Youtube channel if you are interested in more than my summary! But one of the lines I liked the most was that the story of early medieval Argyll is told through three overarching narratives all of which contain the arrival of someone: the arrival of the Scots of the kingdom of Dal Riata, the incoming missionaries in The Age of the Saints, and the invasions of the Vikings. As someone who arrived here too I like that. I feel like more and more of my imagining of a narrative of this place is coming to me. Although I have been looking at metal detector rentals online just incase I feel motivated to do some searching!

The Hostage Stone found on the island of Inchmarnock showing a drawing from the late 8th or 9th Century. I love how it looks like the children telling a story. Perhaps that's whose drawing it was!

I'll report back next month.

Much love,
Susie
xx

"There is properly no history; only biography."
—*Ralph Waldo Emerson*

FEBRUARY 2022

The Gardeners Cottage
Argyll's Secret Coast
Scotland, UK

February 27, 2022

Dearest friend,

Fast and tricksy little February! I have barely caught my breath let alone rented a metal detector to have deep and thoughtful adventures in the landscape. If ever there was a month to remind us that the lunar calendar makes so much sense, it's February.

February the changeable, filler month that contracts and expands to fill the gaps in the logic of the Gregorian calendar. There is so much history in the choosing of this modern calendar. Literally hundreds of years of incremental arguments pulling us further and further away from the very predictable natural way--not pretending, not made up--way time moves across our planet through the moon and through most female bodies for a time. I wanted to say "isn't it funny?" But it's not funny. Not at all. It was done on purpose and it was one of the early steps which finds us here, a little at a loss for how disconnected we are as a whole from the planet, what is good for us and each other.

How are you? February has been a hard one. Even before things in the Ukraine hit the news. I try to take it all in once or twice a day, and then give myself a break in the hours between

to keep creating things, growing things, making things that feel additive to this world.

Three tropical storms have blown through in quick succession this month. That's why I tried to capture some of the feeling of it on your envelopes this month. Winds of 40 mph plus seem to be a factor in more days than not. Vicious hailstorms. We lost a few elders in the beech trees during it all.

Auntie still stands in her so perfectly protected spot. BFT the oak tree that loves children is in their little sunken grove by the sea and lost only a few branches so far. I haven't been brave enough to check on the biggest, serious old oak perched on the side of a rock because I am feeling far too fragile to deal if it's harmed.

There are so many lessons from these old trees though as the world of our understanding continues to unravel into more senseless war and politicians who believe the rules don't apply to them despite the will of the people they work for being quite clear. It's all so much. And yet, my favourite words right now. And yet, these elder trees have stood for so much longer than I have stood under them. For longer than the government sits or even the names of the country where it sits sometimes. Those trees that can, persevere. We know now for certain that those trees that can help each other do help. It provides some comfort.

Privileges

My UK passport arrived in the mail this month. I've been a citizen for a few years now, but had never sent away for my passport. Honestly after the cost of getting my citizenship, I really didn't want to give any more money for a few moments! But I finally wanted that loose end tied up and so with a picture that actually looks like me now (unlike my poor Canadian passport photo) it is here. And I have joined the very privileged of the world with multiple citizenships and the doors and choices that gives me.

Wildlife Camera Fun

I had a lovely time again this month with the wild life camera—meaning I set it twice because, February, and I wasn't as ambitious as I could have been! But I was able to capture a species I haven't shared with you yet which is the amazing little pine marten. This little mammal is critically endangered in

He was ready for his close up, but the camera couldn't handle it! I have a video where you can actually tell that it was a pine marten and another shot of its furry belly!

England and Wales. Like all the non-human predators on these islands it has been horribly persecuted. I love that their scientific name is *martes martes* like they are the most marten of the martens. Or if you speak Spanish Tuesday, Tuesday! They need woodland to live though. Healthy woodland not just commercial conifer mono- crops type.

This image is from The Vincent Wildlife trust to show you the real deal.

They can need up to 200 hectacres for a healthy male! They mostly eat mice and voles and many, many berries! (which explains their fondness for jam when left out at wildlife blinds and feeding tables). But they will take birds too when it's easy. One more neighbour to know about and protect. We figure that there were some chickens lost to a pine marten this year, but chickens, no matter how loved, aren't endangered and it's our job to protect livestock and pets we insert into a landscape and not erase naturally occurring predators.

I have tried to put the camera in a better place to get a good portrait as we speak. I put some berries as an offering a little further away to see if I can get the shots before it gets too curious again! I captured a cheerful little red squirrel in this spot too, so I left it some nuts. I'll report back. It gives me joy to see them living their lives away from us.

Returning Light and Indoor Nights

February is the month though that you can feel the returning of the light. It's so wonderful to be able to pop out for a second walk with the creature around 4 or 5pm and not even be close to twilight. It's 6:30pm as I write tonight and the sun is still making the sky glow west of the mountains of Kintyre. But the weather has been harsh so I also gave a substantial portion of my evenings this month to watching Apple's comedy series Ted Lasso. I'm so late to the party, but it was funny and kind, and filled with the characters of men outside of toxic masculinity even in the middle of sports team. Like real life. There is a lot of toxic masculinity about—particularly if you are a single woman of a certain age who isn't open to random men making decisions on your behalf! But I loved it because it reminded me of all the great men I have around me in my life. And I don't think entertainment gives them enough leading roles either. The show made me laugh out loud and cry quite a bit, the good cry, the tender kind. And I just long for more of that content in the world. The ones about us, flawed, a little bit ridiculous, people just trying to remember to try and be a better version of ourselves.

I hope you have come through February intact too! Even if barely.

Much love,
Susie
xx

"So, what do we do? It's quite straightforward. It has been staring us in the face all along. To restore stability to our planet we must restore its biodiversity, the very thing we removed. It's the only way out of this crisis we've created—
we must rewild the world."
- Sir David Attenborough

MARCH 2022

The Gardeners Cottage
Argyll's Secret Coast
Scotland, UK

March 29, 2022

Dearest Friends,

March in like a lion out like a lamb? March is one of those really liminal or in-between months of the seasons here on the west of Scotland. The turning is tangible and you feel like you have just started down the joyous, cacophonous slide into spring and warmer, lighter times.

Here at The Gardeners Cottage I've been blessed with an eruption of beauty in a very warm and dry ending to March. It's been an emotional month holding a lot of contradictory things true at the same time. The carnage goes on around me amidst

Beautiful hellebore! Two varieties are in bloom at the moment and I'm in love with both! I could stare into their centres for days and try and count the orchid spots on their petals. If ever there was a defence of shade these are it!

the several thousand daffodils in blossom here on the estate. Thank you for your beautiful responses to my heartbreak last month, I know you share the care for our natural world with me and we're all just here trying to figure out what we can do about changing course.As always now, nature resets me. Grounds me in the present moment and allows me to be active in making decisions and reaching for the things I want to be true stronger than ever.

For me nature's disinterest in our wars and horrifying treatment of each other is just a confirmation of how meaningless that behaviour is. Spring isn't paused because of the senseless war in Ukraine. The more-than-human world doesn't stop and gasp when we allow violence to overtake us. It moves aside and tries to recover from the lunacy like all the humans impacted but not involved in the conflict do too. What is it about us that we keep creating the conditions for this story to repeat over and over again?

One of the human stories I encountered here in Argyll was that of the painter Tom Shanks. He was a conscientious objector in the second world war. And I think of the bravery it takes to have done that as a young man. The judgement that would have rained down on him and others like him. The atrocities occurring then and now need to be stopped. But I can't help thinking about how do we get to the point where everyday people have to wield the guns to undo or stop something they did not start or want or agree with? Let the leaders engage in single combat if war-making is their aspiration. No more foot soldiers. Maybe it's my age and the fact that I was raised in Canada where this was an important idea that I no longer believe is meant the way I understood, but peace keeping  can never be done with guns and deadly force. That is war stopping. We need better definitions of peace. Peace must be a verb. Why aren't we always making peace? Not just stopping or calming war?

Flowers for your heart

And yet... and yet! Things are so beautiful at the moment. The flowers and blooming things have begun their shameless show.

The next 'most beautiful thing I have ever seen' happens daily at this time of year. It's so very special to watch the world unfurl again. To listen to the soundtrack of new bird pairings and discussion while inspecting nest sites. It's a wonder to see returning species who wintered deep asleep or far away.

The frogs have awoken to their spring spawning responsibilities with enthusiasm. The ducks and geese are back on the loch and ponds searching for the best sites. I thought I would just fit as many of the joyous pictures in as I could instead of just telling you about it all. Let's linger in early spring's gifts for a while.

A very good ending

And the instinct to linger with joy will make even more sense as I write you this next bit. It is with the deepest gratitude and all sorts of feelings that I let you know that I will be retiring Letters from The Gardeners Cottage at the completion of their third year. April 2022's letter will be the last. It feels like such a good time to celebrate the completion of a wonderful project! As best I can tell there have been just shy of 2000 letters sent in that time. I know so many of your addresses almost by heart! 2000 times you have all welcomed me into your homes and inboxes and said that what I was doing these last three years was valuable to you. I can't express my gratitude enough for what that support and connection has meant to me. I know what I was doing at first didn't make sense to a lot of people who knew me, who never imagined I could be so happy alone in this space—always trying to be more alone in the space hahaha! But it has also been so very important to know I am not alone in this craving for a relationship beyond consumption with the natural world. To remember how I was with the more-than-human world when I was a child and try to find it again. To know that you wanted me to share what was happening for me here has been one of the greatest surprises of my life. I'll not forget it.

Those of you that are quite new to me, and a big shout out to those having joined knowing they are part of the unraveling— I'm so grateful for that support too—I'm sorry it has been so little time together. I really didn't come to this decision until just a short while ago. I've known some of you all my life and so many of you started as strangers, but aren't that anymore. I've kept every single letter you've written me back.

As my rewilding has settled and deepened my relationship with the more-than-human world, I have also deepened my relationship and appreciation to my own timings. And I know for certain that this particular project has bloomed for me for now. In fact I will be taking all my lessons of the last three wonderful years and transporting them back to Canada with me (and Alfred of course) later this summer to reroot myself in the lands of my birth.

So next month will be our last together and hopefully a proper celebration of what has been.

Thank you for being here with me.

Much love,
Susie
xx

"It was one of those March days when it is summer in the light and winter in the shade."
-CHARLES DICKENS, GREAT EXPECTATIONS

APRIL 2022

The Gardeners Cottage
Argyll's Secret Coast
Scotland, UK

April 24, 2022

My treasured friend,

Well now that we've got
the big news out of the way

Carraig nom Ban, the rock of the women.

last month, this month we can revel in what this life at and
these letters from the Gardeners Cottage have been for me.

I expected to enjoy my life here at the Gardeners Cottage
and this lifestyle, but your support and response to the letters
have been such a joy and surprise! I've loved that each of you
have found me and that we connected in whatever ways
happened. I've loved knowing you are out there and that there
is a tiny web we've created together of people very interested
in the preservation of the more than human world and the
wildness in ourselves. It's been so good to find you. The world is
designed to make us feel awfully alone in many ways. Building
our web of connection through words and art and flowers and
growing and restfulness is a revolutionary act that I definitely
intend to continue!

I'm so proud of what I've done here. The beauty I've found,
the love, the relationship with the landscape, the stories
coming to me out of the earth and stones all while mostly not
feeling safe here (for human reasons of course). It's quite
miraculous actually. But that's how stories go when they start

with a conversation with the land itself. If you remember the day I viewed the cottage I went for a walk. At the time there was nothing about me that made me the perfect-on-paper candidate of many that were looking to let it.

As I walked I said to the landscape "I love you. If you want me here with you make it happen." And it happened. That's also why I trust it so much that it's time to go now. My vision of being gifted a book in this space has also come true twice over. And I can't write that next book while I'm here. I know that too. I can't be grieving the current woundings of the landscape while trying to tell a story in its deep past. I need to get a little distance, find some safety for that part of me who needs my inquiries not to affect what happens in my house. I need space to process what I've learned here. I need clean water! And I'm fine with that.

Wild enough to go home

Hand in hand with the time to leave this landscape was the desire to return to Canada where I was born. I feel like I've grown myself wild enough to go home. Not tamed or civilised again like the Welsh legend of Mis, but wilder. A little more feral in my soul. Knowing I am meant to be in relationship with the landscape and creatures. I need to hear the coyote call at night in the world and in my soul. I think living here where it is so beautiful and yet knowing how much is lost, I can't not go home and appreciate what is there. And to find my own way to do whatever is my part in keeping it thriving there.

My time with the UK as my home base has been so impor-tant to me. My ancestors called me and I answered. I came and alchemized some of the pain in our bones. I think the reason to return to your ancestral lands particularly if it is from these islands is not to try to turn back time, but to participate in the rewilding of yourself. Learn the plants and the light and the connection to this particular more than human world that all the words you use come from. It's not just an accident what things are named or the way things have been written about this. Let your ears hear the Gaelic and the Welsh and the tangled English next to the

After three years I think I am actually growing lemons! It almost changed my mind about everything. But they are going to a good home.

landscape that birthed them. Seek out the works of those who lived in that space and light for 100s of generations.

Empire would tell you that these words and phrases are intellectual things that apply equally to all things (so they could discount indigenous languages). But they aren't. They came from here. From this landscape. These waters. This relationship with and as this ecosystem. When colonialism forced others from their words it also distanced it's own people from theirs. If you take your words with you to a new land you won't be lonely for this one. Reweaving the tearing of the land from the words is what we are seeking. It's the buried treasure right before us. It's not the green beer and kilts you want. When we learn what is missing in us and recognise this is what was taken from us as we were deployed as weapons in colonialism, we can arrive with a much different attitude in the places we find ourselves.

And I couldn't have gotten to that place where I feel like I might be additive to that space if I hadn't had this time at the cottage learning how to be myself again. How to truly care about myself. These three years of quiet and solitude allowing me to also notice and unpick how much of my life was on auto-pilot for abandoning myself and my wants and needs because I assumed the abandonment was going to be asked of me anyway. I learned how consistently and purposefully I was hurting and silencing myself. I will probably always keep learning this one. But I found a way in this quiet to be good to myself. To understand that my messy kitchen and my body in a swimsuit or an awful photograph are not excuses to be mean to myself.

I know it is a privilege to have had all this time. And I wasted a lot. But I love the idea of being part of a many year journey alongside the fruit trees. I'm devastated at the idea of leaving my apricot and peaches after three years of making them incrementally happier in the indoor space of the glasshouse. Helping the apricot especially come back down from a canopy pushing through the roof to figuring out how to shape it and grow lower. It's not a one and done thing and I learned to love that and it's a lesson I will treasure.

Lessons from The Gardeners Cottage

I thought I would spend some of our last time together sharing what to me have been some of the most important lessons from my time here.

1. Maybe it's because I've been the quietest I've ever been in my life, but here I've really learned how much our human

sounds travel when I choose to be silent. How even here in the calm and peace I am currently listening to a jet overhead and a car a mile away making its way down the estate road. I can hear a chainsaw or a boat engine from across the loch some days. I learned to hear the estate manager and the game keepers moving around the land so I could go a different way. I felt like prey sometimes escaping the noise. How much have we made the rest of the world adjust to us?

2. I never wasted a moment of time just sitting still on the ground somewhere outside. In fact these were and remain the best part of my day. A warm rock, a hillside, the bench I hauled down a trail so I could sit next to BFT the oak tree.

3. I overcame the challenge of ticks! It was real. The first couple of months were horrific. It felt like they were everywhere. I got bit a few times and Alfred (even with his tick killing meds) got bit many times. But soon you learn to tuck your trousers into your socks while you are walking and do a little check after you've been reaching into trees and bushes. You learn that socks and sandals are for a different time and other walks. You change the dog's medicine to a repellent and surrender to the chemical whose benefit outweighs the risk. And you get on

4. I've learned the names of things. And it has become more and more important to me to do so. What is that tree? That grass? That flower? Which bird makes that song? What's that bug? By being interested in getting intimate enough with them to know them I noticed so many more differences, uniquenesses in things. There is no longer seaweed, but bladder wrack and egg wrack and channel wrack and pepper dulse and sugar kelp and so many

more! Next time you are outside, stop. Look around and see what you can name specifically. Don't worry if it's not very much or maybe you are already wonderful at it. When I arrived here I found myself much more deficient than I thought I was! So I got curious. I have the pile of books and the plant ID apps on my phone to prove it. In one of the early letters I think I said I wanted to learn 100 new things that year. And I've no doubt that I've done that and much more. Often some of my loveliest pictures have just been so I could do the identification later when I was home!

5. I learned how to be trustworthy enough for two generations of robins to come to my hand to eat. The biggest compliment I've ever been given.

6. I've learned the rhythm of my creativity and the support that I give it by doing things over and over. Committing to creating these letters every month for 36 months has been the most consistency and attention I've given my creativity in my adult life. And it has changed me completely for the better. I feel like this has very supportively established the flow for me and that all I've always been dreaming of doing is completely possible. I know it's one of those things that make you want to strike the person who says it... but you have to actually do it. Whatever that thing is you want. Of course you can do it, if you start. You run a marathon by taking the first further walk. Same with writing and making and growing. Trying is the bravest and most rewarding thing you can do.

7. I learned my own pace. Not a surprise that there is another thing we can find wrong about ourselves is our own pace. That if we don't walk up the hill or across the rocks as quickly or as gracefully as someone else it is not

worth doing at all. Another awful thought that our world creates for so many people with different kinds of bodies or wellness or fitness. I have been everywhere on these hundreds of acres of Ardmarnoch. And I have done it slowly and on my butt where needed because my knees or balance doesn't make me very safe. I stop a lot and let myself breathe loudly and be completely winded. And I get everywhere I want to go. It's only when visitors came to walk with me that I noticed I was finding my pace so wrong. I'm getting better at keeping to my own pace in company and helping others do the same.

8. I also learned to stop. Stop and feel the sun. Stop and listen to the wind in the trees above you. Stop and look at what's happening underneath you. Stop and find where that gorgeous smell is coming from. Stop and hear the birds telling each other what you're doing when you come to fill up the feeder. Stop and exhale. Stop and dwell in a particularly magical spot. Stop thinking "I'm not part of this." Our world has been designed to keep going and where and when you choose to stop has a lot of meaning.

9. I've gotten so much better at setting personal boundaries and being curious when I wouldn't or couldn't set them. Knowing what you want and need is so important. Asking for it essential. Conscious compromising with your own consent, empowering. Sovereignty has been a big word for me for a few years and I truly lived it in many ways here for the first time. I truly lived it in many ways here for the first time.

Nature is the most truthful thing in our world

The number one lesson I've learned here is that if we listen to the ecosystem we find ourselves in, this planet, it will give to us generously, repeatedly. And make no mistake we can just keep taking from it and think we know what's best and get a lot for a time. But, that time is limited and we are the ones on the edge of that limit. By 2030 this world is going to be in quite a mess. Unless we learn to listen. Notice what she has to give us and not just what we want. Oh my goodness isn't this also the human lessons we are learning right now too? That we must understand the unique amount each of us have to give the whole and not demand it be the same shape as our own. Some people have nothing to give right now, just like some land-scapes. They need support and time to recover. We should invest in that. Some people have money to give and some people have organisation skills and some have great wells of kindness and empathy. The way we look at nature is the way we look at ourselves, because we too are nature. This needs to be the age of questioning and evaluating not just our productivity, but our impact on each other and this whole planet.

So here we are at the end. How could we have known at the beginning of this three year project what ride we would all go on? I'm just so very grateful that you have been here for some or all of it with me. I know for sure that you have given me support and encouragement and inspiration over and over again during what have been some of the most challenging years in our world. Thank you for letting me be part of your world at this time.

Until we meet again.

Much love,
Susie (& Alfred)
xx

"The only way to know 100% that good is happening in the world is to make sure it's happening around you."
-ME

THE ART OF AN ENVELOPE

Even before moving to The Gardeners Cottage I had always loved to draw on my envelopes. Why should the pleasure of reaching a letter only start when you open it? Why not send a potential moment of imperfect joy or a smile to everyone that touched the letters as they make their way around the world? The wonderful woman at my local post office would often caress the pile while she checked to "see what you have done" this month before dropping them into the post bag. I hope their whimsy adds some joy to your experience as well.

May: Swallows come home.

June: Cutest lambs.

July: Golago come in for dinner.

August: Leaf printing   September: Otter

October: Mushroom

November: Rock Art

January: Robin

February: Windswept trees.

March: Making up bugs!

April: Windswept me.

Make sure you have the complete set!

All three years of letters are now available in book and ebook form wherever books are sold online or direct from the website:
SLSourwine.com

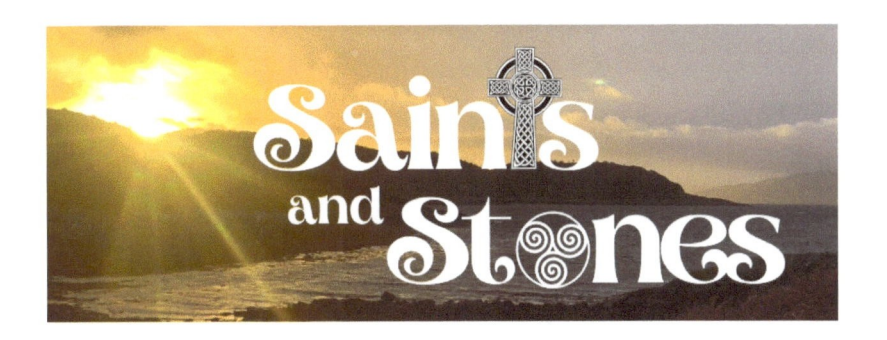

Want more of ancient Scotland inspired by the landscape around The Gardeners Cottage? Subscribe to my newsletter and be a part of the process of the novel coming to life in real time.

History, archeology, dreaming, landscape, myth, and mystics are all inserting themselves in the weaving of these tales. Expect rabbit holes of research, shared chapter drafts, character profiles, research learnings, some artwork that can be part of my creative process, maybe interviews, podcasts and random virtual events.

https://saintsandstones.substack.com

CPSIA information can be obtained
at www.ICGtesting.com
Printed in the USA
LVHW072337110523
746709LV00001B/3

9 781999 885106